CW01213032

Original title:
Popcorn and Limericks

Copyright © 2025 Creative Arts Management OÜ
All rights reserved.

Author: Dean Whitmore
ISBN HARDBACK: 978-3-69074-067-8
ISBN PAPERBACK: 978-3-69074-353-2

Rhythms That Burst and Settle

In a pot of hot kernels, they dance,
Hopping about, they prance.
With a pop and a crack,
They gather some snacks.

A Chewy Chew of Wit

A fellow with jokes, oh so cheesy,
He tickled my ribs, made me uneasy.
With a twist and a grin,
He captured my chin.

Lightearted Puffs of Prose

A jolly old chef, bold and spry,
Tosses in flavors that fly high.
With a sprinkle or two,
Laughter brews through.

The Flavorful Jests of Life

Life's like a bowl of delight,
Surprises and giggles take flight.
With each bite, a chuckle,
In every fun huddle.

Tantalizing Tales

In a pot so big and round,
Bouncing kernels make a sound,
They jump and dance with glee,
Pop! What a sight to see!

Butter drips like melting hopes,
As laughter twirls in joyful ropes,
Each crunch a crazy cheer,
With every bite, we persevere!

A man in a hat quite tall,
Decided he would host a ball,
His guests were all quite neat,
Sipping sodas with their treat!

Tales of pranks and silly tricks,
While munching on their tasty picks,
They rolled and tumbled on the floor,
For fun like this, who could ask for more?

The Jolly Kernel

In a pot, they jump and twirl,
With a hop, a dance, a swirl.
Each crackle brings a cheer,
A party drawing near.

Golden puffs, they rise high,
Bouncing like clouds in the sky.
Their joy is hard to contain,
A laughter like summer rain.

Delights in a Ding

A sound that's crisp and bright,
Brings smiles in the night.
Little treasures start to gleam,
Like dreams from a whimsy team.

With each bite they crack and pop,
Funny moments never stop.
A handful fills with glee,
Tickling taste buds with glee.

Nimble Nibbles

Tiny shapes with lots of flair,
A sprinkle of joy in the air.
They tumble and roll with grace,
In a dance, they find their place.

They jump from bowl to hand,
In a playful, silly band.
Each crunch is a little jest,
Making munchers feel the best.

The Playful Snack

A colorful mix of fun,
These little bites weigh a ton.
Tickling noses with delight,
A crunchy joy, oh what a sight!

Jesters in a crunchy tune,
They'll make you laugh by noon.
A wave of giggles in each bite,
Making every moment bright.

Rhyme Flavors in Airy Delights

In the kettle, things go pop,
Chasing laughter, they never stop,
A sprinkle of cheer,
In each bite we hear,

Silly jokes that make you hop,
Crunchy tales that always swap,
Twirling in the air,
With joy everywhere.

The Joyful Crackle of Stanzas

Hear the sound that brings a smile,
With each chomp, let's stay a while,
Jiggling in your seat,
This snacking's quite a feat,

Witty lines that swirl and pile,
Mischief dancing with style,
A giggle or two,
As the flavors accrue.

Snackable Lines of Enchantment

A comic crunch fills the bowl,
Telling tales from the soul,
Tickle your taste,
No moment to waste,

In this feast, let's lose control,
Every bite plays a role,
Churning with glee,
What fun it can be!

Morsels of Fun in Every Line

Each nibble brings joy anew,
Like a rhyme that sings for you,
Sprinkle in some cheer,
Laughter is near,

With snacks around, we pursue,
All the giggles that ensue,
Savoring the night,
With flavors so bright.

Laughter in Every Bite

In a bowl of golden puffs,
Giggles float like fluffy stuff,
Each crunch a joyful tease,
A salty breeze with cheesy ease.

With friends we munch and laugh,
Like silly kids on a playful path,
A kernel pops, we cheer aloud,
In the crunching, we're all so proud.

A Mirthful Delight

A sprinkle here, a drizzle there,
Zany flavors fill the air,
In every bite, a joke to tell,
Each taste a giggle, a ringing bell.

Beware the crumbs that make us laugh,
With every crunch, we take a gaff,
The joy pops out, it can't be tamed,
In our shared feast, we're all unframed.

The Flavor Threads

A tapestry of tastes so bright,
With every chomp, we take flight,
Savory whispers and sweet surprise,
Laughter dances in our eyes.

From buttery bliss to caramel swirl,
Each nibble spins a happy whirl,
We swap our tales while munching free,
In this symphony of glee.

Canvas of Crunch

A canvas painted with crispy glee,
Each bite a brushstroke, wild and free,
We gather 'round with knowing grins,
   As laughter fills the air, it spins.

From sweet to savory, all is fair,
Each crunch, a pop we love to share,
In every morsel, a mirthful spark,
Under the glow, we light up the dark.

Jocular Scraps

In the cinema bright and loud,
A snack so light draws the crowd.
With every crunch, laughter grows,
As silly antics steal the show.

Minds wander while munching away,
Each kernel brings smiles, hooray!
A funny tale in every bite,
Magic moments take flight.

Savoring the Chuckles

A twist of fate, a giggle or two,
As flavors burst, it's a joyful brew.
Friends gather round with glee so wide,
In this feast of jest, they all abide.

Stories tumble, oh what a spree!
The more they snack, the funnier they be.
Laughter rings, like bells, it soars,
Sharing bliss, as humor pours.

Whimsical Nibbles

Tiny bites with a comical flair,
Each chip and crunch fills the air.
Silly sounds that tickle the ear,
Joyful munching, spreading cheer.

Laughter bubbles like fizzy streams,
As funny tales dance in dreams.
With every giggle, the fun is grand,
Mirth and munchies go hand in hand.

A Symphony of Crunch

In the theater's glow, we sit in rows,
Nibbles crunch, and laughter flows.
Chewy tales wrapped in delight,
Tickling noses, oh what a sight!

Comedic plots take us by storm,
Each munch a giggle, each crunch a norm.
And as the story twists and twirls,
Joy erupts in happy whirls.

Flavorful Quips

A kernel jumps high, what a sight,
Popped with a crack, pure delight.
With butter dripping, oh so grand,
In every bowl, a taste so planned.

Joked with a crunch, a joke anew,
Tickling noses, laughter ensues.
Flavors that dance and waltz in the air,
Each munch a riddle, a giggle to share.

The Silly Snack Journal

Once in a bowl, a popcorn tale,
Of feathers and friends, who sat on a rail.
They cracked silly jokes, amidst all the fun,
While sharing their treats, oh, the laughter begun!

With every pop, there came a new jest,
A roast of a nut who thought he was best.
But soon all would see, with a crunch and a cheer,
That joy is the flavor that draws us near.

Tales from a Fond Bowl

In a bowl of joy, the stories unfold,
Of buttery dreams that never grow old.
They whispered sweet secrets, flavors collide,
With airy delights, on a wild popcorn ride!

A pinch of salt, a sprinkle of glee,
Each kernel's a laugh, as lively as can be.
The tales of a snack, the jokes they ignite,
In the heart of the night, oh, what a delight!

Crunchy Journeys

Off on the trails of buttery bliss,
With every crunch, we dare not miss.
Traveling through flavors, both deep and bright,
With giggles and crunches, we soar into night.

Maps drawn with salt, a path of delight,
Each munch a twist, turning wrong into right.
So gather your friends, let's take a ride,
In crunchy adventures, let's take our time!

The Joyful Feast

In a bowl so round and wide,
A crunchy treat we won't hide.
With butter and salt in tow,
We munch and giggle, oh what a show!

Friends gather round, laughter's the key,
Chomping and chewing, wild as can be.
A sprinkle of joy, a dash of cheer,
With every bite, happiness is here!

Crisp Mirth

Bright kernels dance, they pop and sizzle,
A laugh erupts, it's quite the drizzle.
Toss 'em high, catch them with glee,
Each crunchy morsel feels fancy and free!

From old tales told, we chuckle and snort,
As buttery flecks roll in with a sport.
For every crunch, a giggle we trade,
In this tasty game, our worries just fade!

Whimsical Snacking

In a whimsical world where snacks do play,
Joyful nibbles chase worries away.
With flavors that tickle, both sweet and bright,
Every bite brings laughter, pure delight!

We share silly stories, we chuckle and chime,
Floating on laughter, losing all time.
The more that we munch, the funnier it gets,
In this merry land, no regrets or debts!

Lighthearted Treats

A dance of flavors, a sprinkle of fun,
As kernels pop, joy has begun.
With each silly crunch, our spirits rise,
In the theater of snacking, we're the stars in disguise!

So gather the crew, let laughter ignite,
As we savor each munch, from morning till night.
With a giggle and crunch, we cheerfully feast,
In a merry land where fun never ceased!

Jests in Every Crunch

In a theater dark and wide,
A crunch echoes far and snide.
With each little pounce,
Laughter does bounce,
As munchers giggle side by side.

The kernels leap, oh what a sight!
Dancing around in delight.
With every loud pop,
The chuckles won't stop,
A riot of flavor takes flight.

The Snack that Sings

There once was a treat so sweet,
It could make your heart skip a beat.
With a crunch and a cheer,
You'll want it quite near,
As it taps out a jolly beat.

With flavors that spark and ignite,
It sneaks in your dreams every night.
In bags tightly sealed,
Its magic revealed,
Each munching brings pure delight.

Flavorful Fables

A tale of a snack, bold and bright,
That glided through shadows at night.
It whispered sweet lore,
With a crispness galore,
And turned every bite into light.

With wisdom from kernels once grand,
It journeyed across popcorn land.
Each munch held a jest,
A riddle engrossed,
In laughter, the snack took a stand.

Crispy Rhymes

In bowls piled high, a feast grows,
A joyous parade of crunch flows.
With flavors that sing,
And joy that they bring,
Each nibble a burst that glows.

These bites spin a yarn, light as air,
With giggles and relish to share.
Through crunches and munches,
With laughter, it punches,
A symphony airy and rare.

Fables in Each Bite

A kernel danced, oh what a sight,
With tales so quirky, pure delight.
They popped and spun, in cheerful rhyme,
Creating laughter, one bite at a time.

A crunch so crisp, it whispered low,
Of heroes bold and tales we know.
With every munch and every crunch,
Adventures blossom, a tasty lunch.

Flavorful Chuckle

A sprinkle here, a dash of glee,
Each nibble tickles, can you see?
With smiles wide, we share the joy,
As flavors frolic, oh what a ploy!

The laughter bursts, like buttercream,
In silly thoughts, we all can dream.
Nibbles giggle, crunches tease,
With every bite, we aim to please.

Festive Crunches

Gather 'round for a cheerful feast,
With merry nibbles, laughter increased.
Each crunch a giggle, so full of cheer,
Join in the fun, the friends are near!

A handful tossed, a smile ignites,
With silly tales that spark delight.
Each crunch a story, a twist or two,
Let's munch together, me and you!

Tongue-in-Cheek Treats

With jokes a-bubbling, flavors blend,
Each bite a wink, a twisty trend.
Crunchy whispers, they make you giggle,
As flavors prance and laughter wiggle.

A pinch of mischief, a laugh divine,
In every handful, the joy will shine.
Together we crunch, together we joke,
For moments like these, we happily stoke.

Savoring Smiles

In a bowl of joy, they gleam,
Popping up like a happy dream.
With every crunch, a giggle starts,
Tickling the funny bones and hearts.

Each bite a tale, light and airy,
Making moods bright, never dreary.
Crunching loud with all the zest,
Life's little crunch, we know it best.

Gather friends for a tasty show,
Laughter shared, in a friendly flow.
Sprinkled with cheer, just take a chance,
Join the feast, let your spirit dance.

Crunchy fun fills the night,
Every laugh, a perfect bite.
In each nibble, we find delight,
A merry munch that feels just right.

The Flavorful Fable

Once a kernel, shy and small,
Dreamed of fortune, fame, and all.
With a pop, it took to flight,
Becoming magic, pure delight.

Friends gathered round to cheer and munch,
Stories spun with every crunch.
Flavor dancing, hearts ablaze,
Their laughter sparkled, brightened days.

Chasing crumbs that flew away,
Silly antics led the play.
Each tale had a twist of fun,
In this feast, all worries shun.

We shared the tales from start to end,
Memories made, and joy to lend.
Gather close and take a bite,
Life is grand with shared delight.

Soundtrack of Crisps

A symphony of crackling cheer,
Each note poppin' loud and clear.
With every nibble, laughter roars,
Drawing smiles from all the floors.

Dancing crumbs in the breeze,
Tickling toes and giggling knees.
Happiness in every bite,
A crunchy tune feels so right.

Melodies of flavor blend,
As laughter swells, no need to mend.
Each kernel plays its funny part,
Playing tunes straight from the heart.

So gather 'round, let's make some noise,
The joy of munching brings such poise.
With every crunch, the songs unite,
A tapestry of laughs, so bright.

The Frolicsome Bite

In a bowl of cheer, oh what a sight,
Jumps of joy in every bite.
Savoring fun that fills the air,
With silly giggles everywhere.

Light as air, yet bold in taste,
No room for worries, none to waste.
Crunch and munch with hearts alive,
Together in this jolly dive.

Craving laughter, never shy,
With each nibble, oh me, oh my!
The frolicsome bites we share so fine,
Full of mischief, like sweet sunshine.

Join the circle, don't be late,
The joyful crunches celebrate.
In every delight, the laughter's bright,
A crunchy giggle is pure delight.

The Cheery Toss of Light Words

In a bowl of laughter, we find,
Flavors popping, oh so kind.
Jokes and jests, a happy treat,
Crunchy giggles, can't be beat.

With a sprinkle of whimsy, we play,
Witty tales tossed our way.
Each chuckle puffs, oh what fun,
A shared delight for everyone.

Bubbles of joy, they soar up high,
Each quip dances, reaching the sky.
Together we munch, oh what a cheer,
Snappy banter, bringing us near.

As the lights twinkle, the jokes will flow,
Brightening spirits, putting on a show.
So gather around, let laughter ignite,
In this merry mix, everything's bright!

Lively Burst of Tasty Tales

A crunch of stories fills the air,
With each crisp, joy is everywhere.
Tales that tickle, or maybe tease,
Laughter bubbling, sure to please.

Each tale a treat, playful and sweet,
Fleeting moments, we can't repeat.
Jests like candy, a colorful fling,
Moments of mirth that make us sing.

As the rhythms pop, and laughter flies,
Each little nugget, a sweet surprise.
With friends beside, the fun never ends,
Crafting a world where humor blends.

So take a bite of these vibrant spins,
Join in the fun, where everyone wins.
A feast of joy, we gather and share,
With each burst of sound, we light up the air!

Smiles Served in Lyrical Bites

Nibble on smiles, just take a tease,
Each quirk comes wrapped in giggle leaves.
Flavorful banter served with a grin,
As we sit back, let the fun begin.

One quirky tale leads to another,
Each line a laugh, like no other.
Bouncy phrases, short and sweet,
Tasting happiness with every beat.

Mirthful munches, a flavor parade,
Crafted concoctions, never fade.
Friends gather round, excitement grows,
As stories pop, like kernels in rows.

So raise your voice, let laughter flow,
In this whimsical world, let smiles show.
With every crunch, our spirits lift,
Each tasty bite, a joyful gift!

The Frolic of Tidbits and Tones

Tiny treasures of wit unfold,
A sprinkle of joy, bright and bold.
As we nibble on whimsical bites,
Laughter erupts, lighting up the nights.

Rhythmic tales bounce from ear to ear,
Whirling around, spreading the cheer.
Each tiny nugget, a spark divine,
A chorus of chuckles in perfect line.

So gather your friends, don't delay,
Each morsel shared makes the best play.
With every pop, a new laugh ignites,
Creating memories full of delights.

In a bowl of humor, we find our way,
Tasting each giggle, come what may.
This frolic of fun, let it be known,
Together we shine, never alone!

A Crunchy Symphony of Verse

In a bowl where kernels play,
They tumble, leap, and sway.
With every crunch, a giggle flows,
As munchkin melodies do compose.

A show of flavors, bright and neat,
A dance of snacks with every beat.
Butter drips in joyful streams,
While laughter stitches up our dreams.

A crackle here, a pop over there,
Eager hands reaching everywhere.
The rhythm's wild, the humor's sweet,
This crispy treat can't be beat!

So gather 'round and have a bite,
Join the fun, it feels just right.
With every crunch, we all will cheer,
For this nutty symphony, my dear!

Kernels of Joy in Rhyme

Tiny morsels full of cheer,
Whispers of laughter draw us near.
Each kernel a joke, each bite a jest,
In this tasty comedy, we're truly blessed.

With a pop and a fluff, they leap and play,
Creating smiles on a rainy day.
Savory, sweet, a crunchy delight,
Every handful sparks pure delight.

Chomping down with giggles loud,
We wear our fun like a fluffy shroud.
Joy bounces high with every crunch,
A feast of giggles awaits our lunch!

So hand me a bowl, let the laughter flow,
Together we'll share the joy we sow.
In this silly banquet of flavors and glee,
We'll tickle our tastebuds, just you and me!

The Whimsical Popping Dance

A pop! A crack! A burst of flair,
A dance of joy floats through the air.
With each leap, a chuckle rings,
As we cheer for all the silly things.

Round and round the bowl we spin,
Each crunchy treat makes us grin.
Like cheerful dancers, they jump and prance,
Crispy delights lead the joyous dance.

Yellow and fluffy, strange and bright,
They bring such laughter, pure delight.
A merry tune in every bite,
Tickling senses, morning or night.

So join the fun, don't be shy,
Let giggles soar and spirits fly.
In this popping, crackling, raucous cheer,
Every kernel sings, "We're glad you're here!"

Laughter Between the Flavors

In a bowl of joy, we take a seat,
With crispy wonders, oh what a treat!
Each flavor popping, tickling our taste,
As laughter and crunch never go to waste.

Sweet and salty, they play a game,
Making fun of boring names.
A chorus of chuckles fills the room,
With each silly bite, we banish gloom.

A dash of humor, a sprinkle of cheer,
These lively snacks draw us near.
From tangy twists to buttery bites,
Together we share our silly nights.

So lift your hands, let smiles flow wide,
Join this tasting, side by side.
For in this bowl of crunchy delight,
Laughter and flavors take perfect flight!

Bouncing Bits of Bliss

In a pan, they jiggle and dance,
Golden orbs take every chance.
With a pop and a giggle,
They give quite a wiggle.

Friends gather round, what a sight!
Crunching and munching with delight.
They fly in the air,
A whimsical flair.

Between bursts of laughter we share,
Nibbles that float through the air.
A tasty ballet,
That brightens our day.

They flip and they soar, pure bliss,
Each kernel's a jovial kiss.
With flavors that tease,
They aim to please.

Nibbles that Narrate

Beneath the moon's silvery hitch,
They tell tales with a playful glitch.
With a crack and a pop,
The stories won't stop.

A munch narrates joys and woes,
Of rivers, and trees, and snows.
Each bite a fresh plot,
Brimming with what,

While friends share a fit of glee,
Every nibble is full of esprit.
The laughter ignites,
Under starry nights.

So gather around, don't be late,
These stories are simply first-rate.
With each little crunch,
We feast in a bunch.

A Crunchy Ballad

In a pot they jump and jive,
Creating a scene that's alive.
Each sound an old tune,
A festive festoon.

With smiles that gleam bright and wide,
They gather our laughter inside.
With bites full of cheer,
Friends gather near.

A song made of munches and shrieks,
Each flavor a tale that speaks.
Between each sweet crunch,
We savor the lunch.

So let's raise our bowls high and sing,
These treats are a marvelous thing!
With joy in the air,
Life's simple and fair.

Tales to Chew On

In a bowl, they tumble and play,
With each burst, they brighten the day.
They pop into view,
As stories ensue.

A tale of a knight and his quest,
In the land where the flavors invest.
Each kernel a clue,
With laughter anew.

The crunch of the tale has begun,
Filling hearts with sweet, silly fun.
With every loud pop,
The giggles don't stop.

So come join the feast, don't delay,
These moments of joy lead the way.
With each tasty bite,
Life's a delight!

Kernels of Joy

In the pot, they jump and dance,
Golden treats that make us prance.
With a pop and a zing,
They'll make your heart sing.

Butter drizzled, flavors galore,
Munching loud, we always want more.
Each crunchy bite brings a cheer,
Laughter bubbles, not a fear.

Tossed in spice or sweet delight,
Savoring joy from day to night.
Friends gather 'round, smiles all wide,
In this bowl, the fun can't hide.

Little bursts of happiness here,
Crunchy whispers, so much to cheer.
In this feast, let problems flee,
Together we laugh, wild and free.

Giggles in a Bowl

Round and round, the joy does spin,
Tiny bursts that cause a grin.
With twinkling eyes, we share this treat,
Each kernel's laugh is oh-so-sweet.

A sprinkle of salt, a dash of fun,
Under the bright and shining sun.
In this bowl, we tell our jokes,
With every crunch, laughter provokes.

From the kitchen wafts a waft of glee,
Gathered friends, hearts full of spree.
Every nibble brings a giggle,
Joyful moments, never a wiggle.

Pop! Pop! Those giggles grow,
A warm, friendly atmosphere we sow.
Together we munch, toss, and cheer,
In this bowl, the fun's always near.

A Toss of Treats

In a bowl, a clamor and clatter,
Friends grab handfuls; what's the matter?
For every crunch, a laugh will ring,
It's the jolly joy that we all bring.

A twist of flavor, a dash of cheer,
With silly faces, we draw near.
Crispy bites make the fun explode,
Laughter's music lightens the load.

Here's to sharing the tasty bliss,
Every tummy begs for a kiss.
Tossing treats and tales anew,
In the circle of laughter, just us few.

Squeals of joy, like popcorn pops,
In this moment, our fun never stops.
Let's giggle, munch, and spread delight,
With every crunch, the world feels bright.

Cheery Chews

Little munchies bring such cheer,
Each bite is a bit of fun, my dear.
With quirky flavors, we explore,
Laughter bubbles, who could ask for more?

Gathered together, the moods alight,
Every mouthful feels just right.
Silly jokes and stories to share,
In this happy circle, we have flair.

Crunching loud, the joy takes flight,
Warming hearts through day and night.
As we chew, the smiles abound,
In this playful dance, bliss is found.

With every chew, a silly rhyme,
Laughter dances, perfect time.
Let's keep munching, let's not rue,
In our world of cheer and chew.

The Taste of Poetry Unfolding

A crispy crunch in the air,
Words bounce, hop, and flare.
Beneath the surface lies delight,
Each syllable pops in the night.

With every nibble, a laugh will bloom,
Verses dance in the room.
A sprinkle of joy, a dash of cheer,
These tasty lines bring us near.

The flavor of whimsy fills the void,
Our spirits giggle, never annoyed.
Each twist of phrase, a playful tease,
Igniting joy with effortless ease.

In this bowl of lyrical treats,
Every line brings its own beats.
So grab a handful, twist and twirl,
Let your laughter unfurl.

Spirited Seeds of Creative Whimsy

Sprinkled in a fizzle of fate,
Ideas bubble, can't wait!
A giggle bursts with every crack,
Imagination takes a whacky track.

Scattered seeds of cheer unfold,
Crafting stories bright and bold.
Each little pop fuels the dream,
As laughter flows, like a stream.

We take a ride on a fluffy cloud,
Where humor shines, strong and loud.
Twists of nonsense join the play,
Filling our hearts in a jolly way.

So come along for the poppy treat,
With every line, we feel the beat.
Embrace the laugh, let go of the stress,
In this world of whimsy, we are blessed.

A Snack for the Soul's Imagination

In a bowl of dreams so bright,
Snack away, take a bite!
Each morsel holds a silly jest,
Tickling minds, it's for the best.

Laughter lingers, flavors collide,
Words cascade and they slide.
With every crunch, the giggles soar,
Infused with joy that we adore.

Whirling thoughts like fluffy fluff,
In a world where jest is enough.
So share a smile, gather 'round,
In this delight, joys abound.

Each snippet serves a flair of fun,
A laugh to share with everyone.
Taste the rhythm in verses formed,
A playful treat, endlessly warmed.

Kernel Dreams and Poetic Schemes

Dreamers craft with every cheer,
As words pop, we draw near.
Bursting bright with silly schemes,
Nurtured deep in laughter's beams.

With every kernel, tales bloom bright,
Whimsical wonders take flight.
Jokes unfold like petals wide,
In this joy ride, we all glide.

From playful puns to mischievous rhymes,
We dance along the path of times.
In this merry, nutty land,
We find unity, hand in hand.

So laugh and snack as we all roam,
In this poetry we call home.
Embrace the whimsy, take a seat,
For in this fun, we feel complete.

Bubbly Flavor Tales

A kernel danced in the pot,
It popped and gave quite a thought.
With butter it swam,
An unsticky jam!

A bowl filled up to the brim,
With laughter that started so slim.
Crunching each bite,
In pure delight!

The flavors swirled 'round with glee,
As friends gathered close by a tree.
We giggled and cheered,
The mood that we steered!

Each munch brought a chuckle or two,
As silly faces came into view.
With joy in the air,
We bantered with flair!

Grazing on Giggles

A crunchy treat held a surprise,
It made all the munchers rise.
With every great crunch,
Came a wacky punch!

A sprinkle of joy joined the feast,
As silly snickers were released.
From one little bite,
Joy took to flight!

Friends whispered jokes, not so sly,
With each nibble, we burst out in cry.
The room filled with cheer,
As laughter drew near!

Every kernel was puffed up with mirth,
Creating a magical birth.
We chewed and we grinned,
As smiles never thinned!

The Spirited Snack

A whisper of crunch in the air,
Brought giggles that sparkled with flair.
With every sweet pop,
The fun would not stop!

Lively banter danced on the lips,
As munching turned into some quips.
We filled up the bowl,
And laughter took toll!

With flavors that tickled our tongue,
The joy was both sweet and quite young.
We feasted in glee,
So happy and free!

Each bite led to one more delight,
Until the last kernel's flight.
Our hearts light as air,
In the warmth we did share!

Festive Flavor Notes

The scent wafted high as a kite,
Inviting all folks to delight.
With colors so bright,
It felt just right!

We gathered around with a cheer,
As joys came alive, bright and clear.
Each crunch brought a grin,
In the bustling din!

Sharing the laughter and fun,
Brought together all, one by one.
With munches and quirks,
We played silly works!

As flavors exploded and soared,
Our spirits were happily poured.
In this festive space,
We danced with a race!

Eloquent Cravings in Stanzas

In a bowl so round and bright,
Crunchy dreams take flight,
Flavors dance and twirl,
In a joyous whirl.

Jokes collide with cheesy flair,
Lightness floats in the air,
Giggles pop like kernels fun,
Underneath the blazing sun.

Laughter fills the cozy room,
As crunches push away the gloom,
A savory melody sings,
Joy is what this moment brings.

Each bite a quip, a happy tease,
Crispy echoes, playful ease,
Where cravings spark and then ignite,
In this feast, all feels just right.

Whimsies in a Crunchy Wrapper

Wrapped in laughter, crispy glow,
Funny tales begin to flow,
With every crunch, a giggle breaks,
A whimsical dance, our joy awakes.

Twirling flavors, bright and bold,
Stories shared, both new and old,
Every bite, a chuckle's friend,
In this feast, the fun won't end.

Jests unfold in crunchy bites,
Filling evenings, dazzling nights,
Like magic spells with silly charms,
Devouring smiles while we disarm.

Oh, the joy from each delight,
Crinkling wrappers, pure delight,
In laughter's sway, we find our peace,
As whimsies dance, our cares release.

Dance of Delights in Text

In digital realms where fun prevails,
Textual treats and silly tales,
Each character a joyful spark,
Setting off a clever lark.

Witty words just bounce and play,
Creating laughter, come what may,
With every tap a giggle grows,
In the chatter, humor flows.

A tapestry of quirks and cheers,
Filling hearts and brightening years,
As pixels pop with cheeky glee,
This is where we long to be.

Let's dance through words with carefree grace,
In this digital, joyous space,
Where laughter wraps around our hearts,
In the playful rhythm, joy imparts.

Bursting with Humor and Color

Colors burst, a vibrant show,
Joyful moments steal the glow,
Every hue a playful song,
In this feast, we all belong.

With every crunch, a laugh takes flight,
Bright and silly, pure delight,
Crisp sensations spark with cheer,
Cheeky grins to draw us near.

Textures mingle, colors blend,
Humor here is time to spend,
In a riot, laughter streams,
Crafting joy from playful dreams.

So let's indulge in every bite,
A colorful and funny sight,
Together we will surely find,
A burst of laughter, sweetly kind.

Tales from the Snack Stand

In a corner bright, snacks align,
Crackers and candies, all so fine.
A silly ol' man, with a grin so wide,
Tossed jellybeans, and they started to slide.

A lady did laugh, with a twinkle in eye,
As sweet treats began to soar and fly.
Each bounce and each roll brought giggles galore,
Her hat tipped and spun, who could ask for more?

A child grabbed a treat, with a plop and a pop,
The snacks on the floor made everyone stop.
With each little crunch, the laughter would rise,
As chocolate-covered wonders danced 'neath the skies.

So heed the tale, of the stand so bright,
Where joy is unveiled in the munching delight.
With chuckles and chuckles, the snacks take a stand,
For laughter and munching go hand in hand.

A Mirthful Munch

Crunchy delights in a bowl on the way,
Chasing the blues like a game the kids play.
A biscuit did tumble, a chip did glide,
Friends roared with laughter, no need to hide.

A peanut took flight, with a puff and a cheer,
Landing in cheese dip, with grasses so clear.
The giggles erupted, both near and far,
As snacks turned performers in a retro bazaar.

With sprinkles and sweets, each flavor takes flight,
Creating a circus, oh what a sight!
In this foodie delight, whimsy is king,
With voices of joy, the chorus we sing.

So grab your snacks, and take a big bite,
Let your heart dance in the merry moonlight.
Each crunch and each giggle, a memory to stitch,
The laughter of munching, an everlasting witch.

Whirlwinds of Flavor

Around the table, all colors collide,
Sassy and sweet, each one filled with pride.
A whirlwind of taste, spins round and about,
Creating a game, all filled with good clout.

The nachos were dancing, along with the fries,
Like owls in the night with their big bulging eyes.
Giggles did echo as flavors took wing,
With the sound of a crunch, the snack stand would sing.

A salty parade, in a candy array,
Each munch a delight, come join in the play!
Let popcorn take flight, let pretzels unwind,
In the storm of the feast, pure joy we will find.

With laughter and flavor, this tale will unfold,
As wonders of snacking are lovingly told.
So grab a good bite, let the fun now ignite,
In the whirlwinds of flavor, all hearts feel so light.

Crunchy Silly Songs

In a hall full of munchers, a tune starts to play,
From the crunch of the chips, to the sweet candy sway.
A jingle of joy, as the cookies all sang,
With giggles and crunches, let the laughter bang!

A cookie belt dance, right near the snack bar,
With a tap of the foot, spread joy near and far.
The gummy bears cheered, a sight to behold,
As chocolates enchanted with stories retold.

A parade of the flavors, in harmony dive,
With sprinkles and laughter, we feel so alive.
Join in the chorus, let merriment shine,
Where every bite counts, and the joy is divine.

So let's end this tale with a crunch and a cheer,
For snacks and sweet giggles bring all of us near.
In this world of delight, we joyously cling,
To the crunchy silly songs that laughter can bring.

Whirl of Flavor and Wordplay

In a pot where kernels dance,
They swirl and twirl, a merry chance.
With butter drips and salted glee,
A snack-time whirl for you and me.

Jokes pop up like fluffy treats,
With giggles shared in cozy seats.
Every crunch brings forth a cheer,
A playful bite, bring on the beer!

Hilarious tales, lightly tossed,
In laughter's spark, we'll never be lost.
Munch your way through stories bright,
With flavor coats of pure delight.

So gather round for fun and games,
With tasty twists and silly names.
Each burst of joy is a comic gift,
In this crazy snack-time lift!

A Tasty Flourish of Fun

In a bowl of crisp delight,
Flavors mingle, oh so bright.
Tiny puffs, soft as a sigh,
Taking off like clouds in the sky.

With every crunch, a joke unfolds,
Full of whimsy, never old.
A sprinkle here, a dash of cheer,
All around, laughter draws near.

Join the feast, let giggles rise,
With buttery dreams in every size.
A cheeky wit on every bite,
Taste the humor, pure and light.

As we munch and laugh away,
Let the flavors safely play.
In this mix of fun and glee,
Delight awaits for you and me!

The Crunch of Laughter

With every pop a chuckle sounds,
In crispy shells our joy rebounds.
Little puffs that dance and tease,
Bringing smiles with perfect ease.

A comedy with each hearty crunch,
Life's a game and we're the bunch.
Double-dare the flavors bold,
In every bite, let stories unfold.

Giggles burst like shooting stars,
Flavorful jokes left without bars.
So gather close and grab a seat,
As laughter makes our day complete.

In a whirlwind of tasty bliss,
Each savory bite, you won't want to miss.
With jokes and crunch we'll take a leap,
And in this joy, our memories keep!

Buttered Whimsy

A little sprinkle, a joyful sound,
Of soft delights that twirl around.
Kernels popping, laughter flies,
In every space, the fun fills the skies.

Imagine tales that tumble down,
A playful twist with a funny frown.
Each crisp bite brings tales anew,
A whirlwind of what we all can do.

Silly stories, flavors collide,
In every crunch, the joy won't hide.
Let's celebrate this tasty spree,
In buttered whimsy, wild and free.

So hold your snack, embrace the cheer,
With laughter and munching close and near.
In every bite, find delight's embrace,
For happiness grows in every space!

Joyous Noshing

A kernel danced on the hot stove,
It wiggled and jiggled, oh, what a grove!
With a pop and a cheer,
It burst, oh so near!

Flavors all mingled in bright, bold hues,
Each bite a surprise, like quirky views.
Sweet and savory trails,
Winding like funny tales.

Crunching away, the laughter floats,
In a bowl full of joy, with giggly quotes.
Friends gather 'round,
With smiles they abound.

As laughter erupts like the snacks in hand,
What a whimsical feast across this land!
Every crunch a sweet sound,
In this merry-go-round.

Riddles of the Crunch

In a carnival bowl of crispy cheer,
Each snack brings a riddle, oh dear!
What makes the sound?
Is it joy found?

Tiny treasures that gleam and shine,
Their crackle a clue, oh so divine.
With giggles that roll,
And bright, happy soul.

Guessing the flavors like a game of charades,
Playing with munchies, oh what escapades!
A dab of sweet salt,
With flavors that halt.

Laughter erupts with each savory bite,
It's a riddle of crunch, pure delight.
So take a big scoop,
Join the laughter troop.

Cheeky Munching

Nibble a morsel with a cheeky grin,
Each crunch a secret, a sly little win.
A sprinkle of fun,
'Til the day is done.

Winks exchanged with each playful bite,
The snacks all giggle, a silly sight.
With laughter we share,
In the crispy air.

Joyously chewing on wild, quirky dreams,
Every kernel bursting with laughter beams.
With chuckles that rise,
And gleam in our eyes.

As friends gather 'round for this munching spree,
Cheeky delights create harmony.
Our bowls overflow,
With smiles in tow.

Bursts of Delight

In a bowl overflowing with joy so bright,
Each burst a spark, a tickling sight.
Joyful eruptions,
With fun interruptions.

Tasting the magic with every sound,
The giggles bubble up all around.
A surprise in each bite,
What a joyful plight!

Gather the crew for this shared delight,
Crunching together feels so just right.
With tales intertwined,
And hearts all aligned.

Life's simple joys are the best after all,
In a dance of laughter, we rise, we fall.
With every fun pop,
Let's never stop!

Lively Laughter

In a bowl of golden delight,
Little kernels dance with glee.
They pop and skip, oh what a sight,
Sharing joy, wild and free.

With each crunch, a giggle rings,
As flavors burst like playful cheer.
Round the room, the laughter swings,
An echo of fun, loud and clear.

A sprinkle of salt, a buttery splash,
Together they whirl in joyous tune.
The smiles grow wide, all fears can dash,
As night falls down, none too soon.

So grab a handful, don't delay,
Let's celebrate this silly feast.
With merriment, we twirl and sway,
In this chaos, we're the least.

Flavors in Verse

A twist of flavor, a dash of fun,
In every bite, a tale unfolds.
Each little pop, a victory won,
Like secrets shared, never too old.

With cheddar dreams and sweet delight,
A banquet made for giggles and cheer.
Every crunch feels just so right,
A treasure trove of joy, we revere.

The crunch of corn, a rhythm divine,
Each grain a note in this lively song.
With laughter bright, we twist and twine,
In this merry dance, we all belong.

So pass the joy, let laughter play,
In this feast of flavors, we unite.
Each moment adds a joyful ray,
As day drifts into a starry night.

Whimsies of the Day

A kernel leaps, a joyful show,
As whimsy colors every spark.
In the air, good vibes flow,
Illuminating dance in the dark.

Chaotic crunches break the silence,
We giggle, munching with such ease.
It's a playful, crunchy alliance,
Each bite elicits hearty wheezes.

Unruly snacks on a lively plate,
They whistle tunes of happy glee.
With every flavor, we celebrate,
Together, in this pure jubilee.

So chuckle as the night drifts on,
With friends and snacks, we are complete.
In this cozy slice, we've drawn,
Our hearts entwined, our laughter sweet.

A Crunchy Cadence

With each little pop, a sound so bright,
The crunchy rhythm sets us free.
A joyous crackle, pure delight,
In our dance, we find the key.

The flavors bloom, a wild romance,
Salty, sweet, we twirl and spin.
With all our friends, we take a chance,
In every bite, the laughter begins.

A comedy of taste on our lips,
As we share stories and silly jokes.
In this crazy world, we do flips,
Finding joy in all our pokes.

So let's crunch loud, let's crunch proud,
In this circus of flavor, we thrive.
Together we stand, a goofy crowd,
In this heartbeat, we come alive.

Bites of Satire

In a world where kernels dance,
They pop and swirl, given a chance.
With butter drips, oh what a sight,
Each morsel brings pure delight.

The jester leaps with every crunch,
While flavors sprinkle with a punch.
A salty twist, a sweet surprise,
All with laughter in their eyes.

From movie nights to games in tow,
Little hands reach high and low.
A puffy cloud of cheesy glee,
Brings everyone to jubilee.

So grab a bowl, don't be shy,
Let the humor fly up high.
For every bite's a giggle treat,
In this carnival of sweet.

Jolly Inspirations

A kernel's dream is to explode,
With zest and pop on joy's abode.
In theaters where we laugh and cheer,
Each puff's a chuckle, oh so dear.

In cozy nooks, we munch away,
Whispers of jokes in bright array.
With every crackle, sparks of fun,
We gather 'round, our hearts have won.

So here's to friends and silly games,
To bursts of laughter and wild flames.
Each flavor's cheeky, bold, and bright,
They dance upon our tongues tonight.

Let stories blend with joyful sound,
As crispy treasures come around.
A jolly banquet shared with glee,
Together creates our jubilee.

A Taste of Fun

In the kitchen, a quiet pop,
Brings joy that just won't stop.
A frolic of flavors hits the air,
Each bite's a fun, delightful scare.

Around the bowl, we laugh and tease,
Every crunch brings silly breezes.
From butter drips to caramel dreams,
Our laughter bursts at the seams.

With friends who cheer with every munch,
We savor moments, all in a bunch.
It's never dull with snacks around,
In every bite, pure joy is found.

So raise a hand and grab a treat,
Join in the giggles; feel the beat.
For together we shall dive and run,
Into a world full of fun.

Snacktime Chronicles

In the land of flavor, tales unfold,
With crispy secrets, brave and bold.
Each nugget spins a tale or two,
Of adventures ripe for me and you.

As munchkins gather, the laughs ignite,
In buttery bliss, oh what a sight!
Every crunch is a chapter bright,
We spill our laughs, day or night.

With flavors whirling, stories blend,
In savory journeys, we transcend.
The night is young, and joy takes flight,
With every bite, we craft delight.

So let your guard down, take a seat,
For every nibble, life's a treat.
With silly tales from skies above,
Snacktime echoes purest love.

Dreamy Bites

In a world of munchy delight,
Snacks dance in the shimmering light.
Crunch and munch, what a sound,
Joy in each bite can be found.

Flavors pop like stars at night,
Tickle your taste buds, oh what a sight.
Smiles grow wide, laughter flows free,
Nibbling treats, happy as can be.

Every bite brings a youthful glee,
Together, we savor the jubilee.
Crunchy whispers fill the air,
In tasty tales, we joyfully share.

So let's gather around and be bold,
With silly stories of old retold.
In each joyful munch, memories ignite,
Creating moments that feel just right.

Tasty Anecdotes

A tale of flavors, sweet and bright,
Each savory nibble is pure delight.
With a twist of fate, oh what a treat,
In quirky bites, our laughter's complete.

A fellow once dipped a crumpet so high,
It flew from his hand and soared to the sky.
With mirthful giggles, we watched it ascend,
In every bite, a new story to blend.

The cream flew, the jelly did bounce,
Our funny mishaps made us all pounce.
In crumbs and giggles, we found our way,
With memories lasting, come what may.

Each story we share brings us near,
In the warmth of laughter, in joy, not fear.
Tasty anecdotes we parade in cheers,
With every light-hearted laugh, we shed our tears.

Chortles in the Air

In a kitchen bustling, what a scene,
Everyone's laughing, feeling so keen.
Bubbles and giggles arise with the steam,
Chortles and chuckles, like a sweet dream.

With a dash of whimsy and a sprinkle of fun,
We dance in delight, just like the sun.
Every crunch brings a grin to the crowd,
In this joyful chaos, we laugh out loud.

As we gather around, our hearts intertwined,
Sharing the joy, funny stories aligned.
A bit of silliness flying through the air,
With every delicious bite, we banish despair.

So come join the feast, let worries take flight,
In the laughter and joy, we'll shine so bright.
Chortles united, we revel in cheer,
Creating memories with those we hold dear.

.

Medley of Mirth

In a pot full of laughter, we stir up the fun,
With each silly tale, our hearts come undone.
A medley of moments, both hearty and light,
In joyous concoctions, everything feels right.

A friend once tripped, oh what a sight,
Slipped on a treat, in mid-laughter's flight.
With playful spirits, we couldn't control,
Our bellies were aching, our hearts made whole.

We mix up the stories, a twist here and there,
With sprinkles of joy and a dash of fair.
In this whimsical blend, we gather as one,
With quirky refrains, our laughter is spun.

So here is our wish, to keep the charm near,
In a pot of mirth, let's always adhere.
With a sprinkle of laughter and a side of glee,
In this joyful medley, we'll always be free.

The Snacktime Serenade

In a bowl of joy, round and bright,
Little puffs pop, a delightful sight.
They dance and they leap, oh what a show,
Flavors that twirl, a whirlwind glow.

With a crunch and a munch, we all take part,
Laughing and giggling, it's a true art.
Friends gather 'round, sharing the cheer,
Every bite brings more laughter near.

So here's to the snacks, a funny delight,
Bringing us joy from morning till night.
We sing and we snack, such silly fun,
In the land of flavors, we never shun.

Let's raise our bowls! Here's to the giggles,
As we chomp along with wild waggles.
Snacktime is sweet, come join the parade,
In this joy-filled world, all worries fade.

Cheery Compositions

In a bowl of smiles, round and so warm,
Every crunchy piece spouts its charm.
With a pop and a fizz, they play a tune,
A rhythm of laughter beneath the moon.

Sprinkled with salt and sweetened with fun,
Biting in sync till we're almost done.
Every kernel's a joke, every munch a laugh,
A banquet of fun, the cheer we craft.

Gather your pals, share a funny tale,
As we chomp and chew, we'll never fail.
With giggles and giggles, the night is bright,
Our silly sharings take playful flight.

So let's toast to snacks in joyful delight,
Crafting compositions of silly and light.
In this tasty realm, we all belong,
A symphony of flavors, a joyous song.

Revels in a Bowl

In a bowl stacked high, where flavors collide,
Laughter erupts, a joy-filled ride.
Each munch is a smile, bouncing with glee,
Come join the party, there's fun for thee.

With sprightly crunches and chuckles anew,
We toss and we turn, share flavors askew.
The night is young, so let's keep it loud,
Each piece tells a joke, it makes us proud.

Flinging puffs here, there, and everywhere,
Our kitchen's a stage, a lively affair.
With flavors that tickle and jokes that unfold,
Our revelry's sweet, let the fun be bold.

So gather your friends for an evening treat,
With a sprinkle of laughter, it's hard to beat.
A bowl full of wonders, we're never still,
In this sparkling party, we sip and thrill.

The Tasty Troupe

Here comes the troupe, all flavors in line,
Puffing and popping, a tasty design.
Ticklish and tart, a blend so neat,
They shuffle and prance, oh what a feat!

With each nimble crunch, they burst into cheer,
Cradled in laughter, there's nothing to fear.
Friends join the circle, smiles all around,
As giggles and snacks make the best sound.

A pinch of the silly, a dash of the sweet,
Mixing together, they can't be beat.
With jolly delight, we savor the show,
In this festive magic, let the good vibes flow.

So gather your clan for a whimsical night,
As the tasty troupe keeps the vibes all right.
Sharing our bites, joy fills the space,
In this merry moment, let's all embrace.

Verses from a Buttered Bowl

In a theater bright and loud,
A funny fellow stood so proud.
He tossed a kernel high in air,
Landed on a lady's hair.

With laughter echoing around,
He danced like he had just been crowned.
The crowd erupted, tears of joy,
For each silly trick of the funny boy.

His jokes were cheesy, buttery fun,
As giggles burst like bubbles spun.
A mishap here, a stumble there,
The evening ripe with campy flair.

With smiles wide and spirits free,
Life's little goofs were plain to see.
In every crack of mirth and cheer,
The night was bright, no room for fear.

The Sizzling Tale of Mirth

Once a jester with popcorn dreams,
Rode a bike bursting at the seams.
He tried to juggle, fell on his face,
A feathered hat held his grace.

The audience roared, a riotous show,
As he tripped and slipped, oh what a flow!
With each twist and tumble, laughter spread,
Hilarity danced in every head.

A train of giggles rolled down the aisle,
As he waved with charm, a silly smile.
In a world where slapstick reigns supreme,
His antics made hearts distinctly gleam.

With each pop and crack throughout the night,
Mirth spun stories, pure delight.
The jester bowed, with spirits so free,
Leaving joy woven in memory.

Crunchy Muses in a Bowl

In a cozy nook where laughter brews,
Chips and dips get final views.
A poet with an oddball flair,
Wrote verses whilst sitting in a chair.

With bites of crunch, he shared his rhymes,
Between the munching, laughter chimes.
He rhymed about cats wearing hats,
And danced with squirrels and fluffy rats.

Each little nibble sparked a jest,
As ideas churned, he'd never rest.
With a giggle here, a chuckle there,
His quirky verses filled the air.

So gather round, for joy unfolds,
In tales of snacks and antics bold.
With every bite, creativity flows,
In this crunchy haven, anything goes!

Whirlwinds of Delightful Rhymes

In a whirl of giggles, chaos blown,
A poet's mind was brightly thrown.
He pondered puns and clever lines,
Finding joy in quirky designs.

With whimsy painted in each verse,
His thoughts unleashed, a playful curse.
As jokes flew fast like popcorn puffs,
The crowd exclaimed, 'Oh, that's enough!'

He tickled fancy, teased the night,
As laughter bubbled—oh, what a sight!
The more he juggled, the louder his fame,
In whirlwinds of joy, he staked his claim.

So here's to laughter, wide and bright,
In every giggle, day and night.
May the muses dance and jests take flight,
In this whirlwind, all feels right.

www.ingramcontent.com/pod-product-compliance
Ingram Content Group UK Ltd.
Pitfield, Milton Keynes, MK11 3LW, UK
UKHW010926280125
454312UK00006B/49